Parent of an Adult Addict

Hope for the Broken Road

Written by Arlene Boehnlein-Rice

Scripture quotations are from THE HOLY BIBLE, NEW
INTERNATIONAL VERSION®, NIV® Copyright © 1973, 1978,
1984, 2011 by Biblica, Inc.® Used by permission. All rights
reserved worldwide.

Edited by Mary Carlisle Wiley
wileycreativestudio@gmail.com
www.wileycreativestudio.com

Cover Design by Ashley Wells
http://www.31daystowriteyourebook.com/

Dedication

To my most beautiful Gabriel, because of your life my faith has grown to a higher level of hope in Christ. Addiction doesn't win in the end. Christ wins. I am so thankful for the promise to be able to see you again on the other side of eternity. No more tears. No more pain. No more heroin. Until that day, you be a good boy Charlie Brown.

Note to Parents

For approximately fifteen years I have been walking the road of drug addiction with my adult daughter. She has struggled all of her young adult life with substance abuse. Lately, I have received numerous emails and phone calls from other parents asking for advice about how to deal with their adult addict child.

"What should I do? What should I not do? Where do I start? How do I get help for my child? What if they don't agree to get help? How do I get help for myself?" I am asked these questions almost daily. I am not an addictions counselor or a psychologist. I have no expertise in the area of addiction. I am just like you, the parent of an addict.

I am not quite sure why I am being contacted, but I think the calls may have something to do with the fact I have broken my silence. I have chosen to be vulnerable with my family, my friends, my church, and anybody else who will listen to my story. In faith, I have decided to speak out and shed the shame of addiction.

Recently, I attended a women's luncheon on a seminary campus. I sat at a table with eight women I had never met. While sharing prayer requests I mentioned my daughter and her struggle with substance abuse. When the luncheon was over, a beautiful young lady approached me. With a heart overwhelmed with grief, she began to tell me about her brother who recently passed away from a heroin overdose. What struck me was her comment.

"I am surprised you would share about your daughter with us. I wish I was that bold. I've never talked openly to anyone about

my brother here on campus. As a seminary student, I am reluctant to share how my brother died. So I don't mention his death. People would ask why, and I am too ashamed to tell them the truth."

Many others have shared with me their stories and feelings of shame. As you read this book, my hope is you would know you are not alone on this journey. I hope you will gain practical insight into dealing with your addicted child and these pages will challenge you to find a safe place to share your heartache without shame.

These pages reflect the lessons I am learning and the experiences I am having along the journey of being a parent of an addict. I hope the suggestions in this book will help you put the principles into practice, receive support, and help you recognize signs of drug usage.

In the same breath, I recognize there is no magic dust you can sprinkle over the problem to make your child's addiction go away. Your loved one may stay in their addiction no matter the help you offer.

This brings us to you, the parent of an addict. This book offers practical ideas for seeking help and support. As you read the story about my daughter, my prayer is you would ponder the deep question of where you place your hope and peace, even in this difficult season of life. My belief is true hope and peace come from Jesus Christ.

Table of Contents

My Story

The Gasp of Death

He asked me, "Son of man, can these bones live?" I said, "Sovereign LORD, you alone know." Then he said to me, "Prophesy to these bones and say to them, 'Dry bones, hear the word of the LORD! This is what the Sovereign LORD says to these bones: I will make breath enter you, and you will come to life. I will attach tendons to you and make flesh come upon you and cover you with skin; I will put breath in you, and you will come to life. Then you will know that I am the LORD.'"
Ezekiel 37: 3-6

The night was like any other Saturday night, with the exception of having my daughter Lindsay home on a temporary basis. She had been home only a few weeks. Lindsay found herself homeless after depleting all her resources in years of drug crazed madness. Little did I know when I went to bed that night, I would be awakened by a mother's worst nightmare.

Lindsay's substance abuse troubles began as a young teenager. My husband and I attributed her alcohol usage as a phase, a rite of passage. As parents, we did what most parents do when they discover their child is drinking; we punished her, took away privileges, and grounded her. We did not really think Lindsay had a problem. We rationalized, "She is just a rebellious teen." Once our daughter turned eighteen, she moved out on her own. Her substance abuse escalated over a ten year period from alcohol, to marijuana, cocaine, acid, Xanax®, methamphetamine, Oxycodone®,

OxyContin®, and finally landing on heroin.

My husband and I were asleep in bed that Saturday night when we were awakened by a loud, panicked pounding on our bedroom door. My youngest son, Gabriel, was frantic. He had found Lindsay unresponsive in the basement of our home. She had overdosed on heroin; the needle was still in her arm. As a nurse, I immediately recognized her agonal breathing pattern. This type of breathing often occurs in 40% of cardiac arrest patients and is often called the "gasp of death." For 30 minutes, I performed rescue breathing on my daughter. EMS had been called, but got lost on the way to our house. Time was of the essence; every ticking second was a matter of life or death. Statistically, the odds were diminishing with every passing minute. Approximately 20% oxygen was being delivered with each rescue breath, but Lindsay needed 100% oxygen delivery. Access to the necessary oxygen would only be available once EMS arrived with the oxygen tank. My mind haunted me with what each moment meant. If she lived, she would be brain dead or severely incapacitated at best. EMS finally arrived and hurriedly rushed her to the nearest emergency room.

After such a horrific experience, I am graced to say Lindsay is alive today without any neurological deficits or brain damage. She very well could have died. Many who overdose do not live. Gabriel's quick response probably saved her life. He was going to sit on the deck before going to bed the evening Lindsay overdosed, but he said, "Something inside me told me to go see where Lindsay was." I thank God he followed the inner voice.

Why do I share so candidly with you a story I would rather keep to myself? Number one, I am praying my story will help you and others find hope in the gospel of Christ. I pray you will be encouraged, supported, and understood. Number two, I hope these pages will provide direction towards assisting you in seeking out support for yourself. Number three, I felt compelled to speak out after reading an article on LifeWay Christian Resource's blog *Inside Girls Ministry* about a young boy in a church who died from an overdose. Addicts and their families sit in the pews of our churches every Sunday and suffer in silence. The shame and guilt of their child's addiction perpetuate the secret, leaving families overwhelmed, feeling hopeless and powerless.

The very place we should go to seek counsel is overshadowed by fear of judgment and the projection of an image "we have it all together," when we are actually falling apart. God's Word teaches us to encourage one another (2 Corinthians 13:11), comfort one another (2 Corinthians 1:4), and pray for one another (1 Timothy 2:1). There are families dealing with addiction desperately needing support, encouragement, comfort, and prayer.

I have found when I am transparent and risk being vulnerable with challenges I have encountered in life, God uses those opportunities for me to encourage others struggling with similar trials. I hope by offering understanding and support, parents of addicts would be strengthened, knowing someone is interceding boldly on their behalf at the throne of grace before an almighty God (Hebrews 4:16).

Almost four years have passed since Lindsay overdosed. Since then, she has relapsed on several occasions and has spent time in a Teen Challenge® Women's inpatient treatment program, transitioned to a half-way house, worked on the Alcohol Anonymous® 12 Steps, and attended Celebrate Recovery®. Never in my life did I ever think I would find myself thanking God for places like Teen Challenge®, A.A®., or recovery and sober houses. Nor did I ever think I would need the assistance of such places. Today my daughter is drug free for the first time in a long time. Please pray she will remain strong in Christ and remain free from the stronghold of addiction.

What Should I Do?

Part One

Break Your Silence
Seek Help and Support

I vividly remember the overwhelming feelings of powerlessness and hopelessness when I realized the magnitude of my young adult daughter's chemical addiction the Saturday she overdosed on heroin. Sometimes, I have flashbacks of frantically trying to breathe life back into her limp body, her lips blue from lack of oxygen, her face pasty and ashen in color. As a former critical care open heart cardiovascular nurse, I had seen this color many times on my patients who were knocking at death's door.

The experience of Lindsay's overdose has shaken me to the core. I recall having feelings of tremendous shame. Questions pressed me frequently: How do I help my child? Where do I go for help? What are the first steps to seeking help? Who do I tell? Who can I trust?

Before Lindsay overdosed, I sat in the pew of my church silent about how addiction was destroying my family. As a mother, I wanted to protect her from the mark of disgrace which abounds regarding addiction. In society, the stigma of addiction is shame, so I kept silent.

As a parent of an addict, what is your motive for staying silent? Shame was just one of the reasons I remained hushed. As you read my reasons below, which ones resonate with you? Are your rationales similar? What basis are you using to remain tight-lipped about your loved one's drug abuse?

Because of the shame and stigma of addiction.
Because I did not know how to help my child.
Because of denial.

Because I thought I could handle it alone.

Because I did not know how to confront the issue.

Because I did not know how to intervene.

Because I had enabled and thought I was helping.

Because of guilt.

Because of fear. I feared judgment by my family, friends, and church.

Because of feelings of overwhelming powerlessness.

"And because no one loves an addict" (Libby Cataldi, *Stay Close*).

These reasons are prevalent among families of addicts. This is true even in the church. It will be by breaking the silence, dialoguing openly with others walking this trajectory in life, and seeking counsel, we as parents will gain support and help. By discussing our battles, we can learn lessons from each other regarding how to acquire help for ourselves, find support groups, and educate ourselves on how to deal with an addict while striving to maintain healthy lives.

Maybe you are new to this journey or maybe you have been riding the roller coaster of your child's addiction for some time. Whatever your case, one of the most important steps to take is breaking your silence regarding your child's addiction.

One of the biggest regrets I have as a mom of an adult addict is I kept silent for too long. However, I finally sought support. The next few pages will offer you a few suggestions to get you started on the road to breaking your silence.

ONE ON ONE COUNSEL

When my daughter overdosed and was discharged from the hospital, the physician discussed with my husband and me not only our daughter's need to enter an addiction treatment program, but also the need for us to seek help. The doctor's only recommendation for us was to join a 12 Step Al-anon® group. Do not misunderstand, Al-anon® has its place and is a fabulous support group for families. However, I discovered there are other available alternatives as well.

Consider a parent addiction coach

Parent addiction coaching is designed specifically for parents who are dealing with an adult child's drug addiction. This type of assistance is not therapy, but is a support system. A parent coach offers support to help deal with your child's substance abuse. Many parent coaches offer free consultation.

For instance, I recently came across a parent addiction coach, Mike Speakman, L.I.S.A.C, and Director of Speakman Coaching & Consulting. Speakman offers family coaching sessions for parents of adult addicts. I was quite impressed with what I saw on his website. The only problem was, he lives in Arizona and I live in Kentucky. As I browsed his site further, I discovered he provides telephone sessions, so I called him. If you are considering a parent addiction coach, he comes highly recommended. All the information can be found on his website, PAL Group (Parents of Addicted Loved Ones). PAL Groups are support groups of parents of addicted loved ones helping each other. Any parent, anywhere in the USA can join the monthly PAL Group phone sessions for free. I have spoken with Speakman a few more times privately, and have also joined his free monthly phone meetings.

Changing Lives Foundation

The founders of Changing Lives Foundation, Joe and Judy Herzanek, also offer phone counseling to parents of addicts. They have been providing families with addiction needs help for over thirty years. According to Changing Lives Foundation:

"You and your family can work with Joe to formulate a plan which will restore sanity to your life. He will walk you through the steps you need to take, giving you knowledge and support and confidence to do what needs to be done."

I am sure there are many other coaches you could contemplate. Finding a parent addiction coach is one way to break your silence and seek help.

Seek out another parent who has walked this road

Connecting with others who have dealt with a child's addiction is by far one of the best ways I have found to break my silence. There is something about relating with another person who has or is walking in your shoes. I have been able to connect with other families through friends referring me to parents who have a child in addiction, online support, and my church. Since most parents find shame in sharing, there is a reprieve in being able to meet others who are fighting the same battle.

When I worked as an open heart recovery nurse, I remember patients who were petrified before going into surgery. If a patient voiced fears or I sensed their overwhelming anxiety while providing patient education, I would often contact *Mended Hearts*, a support group of individuals who had been through open heart surgery and recovered. This proved to be an anxiety reliever for many patients. Why? Because the patients awaiting surgery could see someone else had been through the surgery and the patient could visualize his own recovery. Patients could ask questions openly to someone who had walked in their shoes. Similarly, seeking out people who are in the same situation as you, dealing with their adult addicted child can be a source of encouragement and wisdom.

Blog or Journal

After Lindsay overdosed I felt like I needed a way to share with other parents, so I started a blog. I realize some are not comfortable blogging. If blogging is not for you consider journaling. The idea is to break your silence by placing your thoughts onto paper or the computer.

Confide in your pastor or local counseling center

When I mustered enough courage and swallowed my pride, I decided to seek help by confiding in my pastor. What a relief to lay bare my shame and need for direction from a person I trusted. My minister referred me to a counselor from another church which offered pastoral care aid experience in substance abuse issues. This was a life saver for me. If you have a minister, consider confiding in him. If you do not, research churches in your area with a pastoral care staff or counseling center which specializes in addiction counseling. You could also contact your local addiction counseling service center and ask for parental addiction assistance. Most offer classes and support for parents.

Consult with your insurance health coach

Another way to receive one-on-one counseling is through your insurance company. If you prefer faith based counseling, you can ask for a list of providers in your area who fall within your network. My insurance, for example, offered to cover 100% of my counseling because I consulted with my insurance's health coach.

GROUP SUPPORT

PAL Parent Support Groups

As I mentioned earlier, PAL Group (Parents of Addicted Loved Ones) is a great resource. I am impressed with the way this group is structured, especially the educational, prayer, and sharing components. What really aroused my interest is the telephone conferences offered once a month. I do not have to leave my home to speak with other parents who have the same struggle. Parent coach, Mike Speakman, joins in on every teleconference call. The monthly group telephone parent coaching is free. When you go to his website, you will find an abundance of resources rich in support and help for parents.

Celebrate Recovery® Support Groups

When my daughter completed her inpatient recovery at Teen Challenge®, she transitioned to a Christian-based sober house. Part of her recovery plan was to attend Celebrate Recovery® meetings several times a week. Since I was unfamiliar with the program, Lindsay invited me to a meeting. I assumed the gathering was for recovering addicts and alcoholics, but what I unearthed was support and help for parents of addicts and people with various hurts and hang-ups. Celebrate Recovery® was founded about twenty years ago by Saddleback Church in California. Senior Pastor Rick Warren wanted to offer a recovery program based upon the Bible, and from his Scriptural research, Celebrate Recovery® was born. The program uses Eight Principles and Twelve Steps, all built on the foundation of the Bible. Celebrate Recovery® can now be found in churches across the United States.

Al-anon®, Nar-anon®, or Families Anonymous®

Probably the most familiar advice you will receive from others is to join an Al-anon® or Nar-anon® group and attend meetings on a frequent basis. Al-anon® family groups hold meetings every day of the week. Members share their own experience of living with alcoholism. The group follows what is called the Twelve Steps. Al-anon® does not offer advice or counseling, but members give each other understanding, strength, and hope. Nar-anon® is similar, but the family groups share their experience living with narcotic addiction of a loved one. Families Anonymous® was developed to help those who love an alcoholic or addict, as well as the alcoholic or addict themselves. Families Anonymous® brings the two groups together allowing open dialogue and support that includes everyone in the family: couples, parents, children, and siblings.

For many months my husband and I attended various Al-anon® groups. At first we were silent and mostly observed how the group was run. We slowly began to learn the ideas, goals, and steps associated with the groups. We were encouraged to "keep coming back." By joining a group you are then encouraged to secure a sponsor and work through the Twelve Steps. Al-anon® allows you to focus on your peace and recovery, not your child's addiction to alcohol or drugs.

ONLINE SUPPORT GROUPS

The Addicts Mom

For several months, I have been a part of a fabulous resource for mothers of addicts called *The Addict's Mom*. The site was developed by a mother of an addict for the purpose of offering an online support group for moms of addicts. It is a safe place where mothers can "share without shame" (plus many other support perks). The site has grown to over 5000 moms and close to 8,000 on The Addicts Mom Facebook page. It is tragic to think of how many families are affected by addiction. The site provides a reprieve for those who are in much need of support and encouragement. This courageous mother, Barbara Theodosiou, began reaching out to mothers out of her own need after discovering her son's struggle with addiction. She has successfully formed a national support group of moms of addicts, and now state chapter groups are popping up and gaining momentum across the nation.

The Addicts Mom holds the goals of allowing parents of an addict to "join with others from your state, seek support, share your story, and make new contacts, gain awareness, and reach out to others who have a loved one suffering from substance abuse." As of today, the city chapter parents corroborate for support and encouragement, raise awareness, and advocate for addiction reform on behalf of their loved ones. This is by far the best support I believe to be on the web for parents of addicts.

Twitter®

Don't panic! We are not talking about hanging your laundry out to dry. Twitter® has some quality support groups in cyberspace. For example, I was scrolling through Twitter® one night and stumbled upon a group chat on addiction.

The way a twitter chat works is through hashtags. You may already be familiar with the use of hashtags when tweeting, or you may be a novice like me and ask, "What is a hashtag?"

For those unfamiliar with hashtags, let me explain: The # symbol is called a hashtag. Hashtags are used to tag key words or topics. When I happened upon the group chat about addiction, I saw #addictionchat attached to tweets, or short updates others had posted, which meant the topic being discussed was addiction.

If you are unfamiliar with Twitter® consider signing up with an account at www.twitter.com. Be sure to check out *Twitter 101* to get you started. Don't be afraid! It really is easy, and can be a great means of support. The chats are hosted by various addiction groups once a week on Wednesday evenings at 9 pm EST.

To join #addictionchat, you'll need to do these things:

1. Tweet #addictionchat by accessing your page and typing your tweet into the white box (once you post it, the hashtag will turn blue).

2. Click on the blue #addictionchat.

3. This will take you to the chat session. Each time you post a chat comment, end it with #addictionchat.

You could also start your own support group chat on Twitter®. For instance, choose a hashtag you would like to use such as, #parentaddictionchat. Decide ahead of time who you will invite and what open ended questions you will ask. Base your questions on what parents want to know. Be specific about the topic, such as "Tonight we will be chatting about enabling." Then, invite your twitter friends or groups to join in on the chat and tell them the time frame the chat will encompass. Another option would be to ask the host of #addictionchat or another respected recovery facility who has a presence on Twitter® to consider starting a chat for parents of addicts.

Facebook®

I have found Facebook® to be an excellent way to join support groups, thus breaking the silence of addiction. At first, I was reluctant because I thought my friends and family on Facebook would receive feeds about the groups I had joined and could possibly see posts. But, I discovered several of the support groups are closed or secret, meaning your friends or family are not able to see posts by you or by others in the group. If privacy is a concern for you, before you join a support group you may want to ask if the group is closed or secret. Here are some of the groups I have joined (There are others, but I am partial to these. Also, you can find links to all these groups in the Resource section at the back of this book):

Addiction Journal
Celebrate Recovery
Heroin Doesn't Care
No Heroin in Heaven
No Longer Bound

Operation 6:12
PAR NKY (People Advocating Recovery Northern KY)
Teen Challenge
The Addicts Mom
The Addicts Mom: KY State Chapter

I am sure there are many other Facebook addiction support and treatment groups. Research Facebook support groups which fit your need then join them and begin engaging with others.

ADVOCATE

It is no secret our children are dying from opiate overdoses. Just pick up the paper, read the news, or flip the channel and you will be bombarded with stories and rising statistics regarding this epidemic. Drugs are in every city, state, suburb, and rural area, and they affect rich and poor alike. Heroin is no respecter of persons. Heroin does not discriminate. Heroin is in every neighborhood. Heroin is making its way into our elementary, middle, and high schools.

Part of the solution to fighting the heroin epidemic is by breaking your silence and advocating for your children. There are numerous ways to become involved. My suggestion would be to find what pushes your buttons and dive into the cause. For instance, when my daughter overdosed and I performed rescue breathing, all I could think was: "I wish EMS would hurry up and get here. She needs oxygen and Narcan." (Narcan/Naloxone is the antidote to an opiate overdose.) Since Lindsay's overdose experience, I have begun researching Naloxone and Good Samaritan Laws.

In a related matter, I just returned last week from an informational meeting about how to participate in addiction intervention laws in my state. I have connected with a group called PAR (People Advocating Recovery). This site allows me to keep up with the latest updates on intervention legislation laws, such as Naloxone and Good Samaritan Laws, as well as other laws which address substance abuse. This group has legislation affiliations in my state, provide information to parents regarding treatment options, and have fought for Good Samaritan and Naloxone legislation in the state in which I live. My current goal is to become Naloxone trained, and then offer my services to train my community in its use and administration. This is only one way in which I have become an advocate.

What if I had access to Naloxone the night my daughter overdosed, but more so, what about other parents? What if other parents of addicts had access to Naloxone and were trained in its usage? Could it make a difference if their child lived or died should she overdose in her parents' home? An even bigger question: Could it make a difference if your child or their friends had access to Naloxone? If your child is going to use, would you prefer their friends leave them, not call 911, or be able to administer Naloxone to your child and call for help? These intervention laws may save the life of your child. Maybe this would be the time your addict child would agree to help. Maybe not, but you cannot save someone who is dead.

Opponents to Naloxone argue by making Naloxone accessible, addicts are encouraged to continue in their abuse. From my experience as a parent of an addict: addicts are going to use whether they have Naloxone or not. By making Naloxone medication accessible, my belief is if an addict overdoses and Naloxone is administered, then maybe, just maybe, they will have a moment of clarity and see their need to enter treatment.

I like how Dr. Jeremy Engel, a proponent of addiction intervention legislation laws, stated his support of Naloxone and Good Samaritan Laws, *"If people fall into the river and they're drowning, I want to pull them out whether they fall into the river again or not."*

Van Ingram, Executive Director of the Kentucky Drug Control Policy advocates for Good Samaritan and Naloxone Laws by commenting, "If they've passed away, there's no chance they'll ever be productive and they leave behind the scars of that."

No Heroin in Heaven advocates by saying, "If they're still alive, there is still hope."

One of the best resources regarding Naloxone and Good Samaritan Laws can be found at the Network for Public Health Law (Look under the Resources at the end of the book under the Treatment Locators and Help section). You can browse the tables and maps and find out if your state currently has Naloxone or Good Samaritan Laws. If you find your state has no such intervention laws, consider contacting your senator and discuss sponsoring such a bill.

Parents of addicts in many states can now ask their family physicians to prescribe Naloxone for them to have on hand should their child overdose. An addict can request a prescription from his family doctor as well. Many cities with strong group supporters, such as PAR NKY, hold Naloxone Training and supply the kits at the training sessions. If you are interested in Naloxone training and obtaining a kit, the first step is to find out if your state has such a law. As mentioned previously, the Network for Public Health Law is a great resource for finding information on your state's Good Samaritan and Naloxone Laws.

Whatever spurs you, be proactive in your pursuit. By being passionate about your cause, you give a voice to your child's struggle and may save a life in the process. If you are unsure, the Internet swarms with parents advocating for their children in various ways. Some parents and advocacy groups hold rallies, plan vigils, plan walks, host music festivals, and use billboards to raise awareness. For instance, No Heroin in Heaven highlights stories of families and addicts to raise awareness of the heroin epidemic.

We, as parents of addicts, desperately need the support of each other, walking side by side, sharing our stories, learning from one another, and encouraging one another. We are stronger in numbers. As you reflect on the tools you have to reach out for support, you are one step closer to helping yourself, and hopefully your child, get their life back.

Educate Yourself about Signs of Drug Abuse

KNOW SIGNS OF ADDICTION

Lindsay's father and I knew she had been drinking alcohol and smoking marijuana. We suspected other drug usage, but we were in denial for the longest time about her addiction. We explained everything away, for the most part, ignoring the signs right under our noses, attributing her usage to normal experimentation. We thought, 'After all, when we were teenagers we experimented with drugs ourselves.' In essence we assumed she could not be an addict because we ourselves did not become addicts. This type of thinking is deceptive.

Once my husband and I became aware of the magnitude, we began to educate ourselves about addiction. We quickly learned signs and symptoms of addiction do not stand alone. In most situations, there are combinations of indications.

What we saw from her opiate abuse were tiny constricted pupils, ashen skin color, dark circles under her eyes, an unkempt appearance, wearing the same clothes for days, drowsy and listless demeanor, small red dots on her arms from injecting, and bruising to extremities (thighs, feet, legs, and neck are common sites the addict will use to inject). There were lies, manipulation, and theft, sleeping for long periods of time, sniffling, and sneezing. An addict once telling me when an opiate abuser is in need of a fix (usually approximately three days from last use) they begin to sneeze, so I began to watch for sneezing episodes.

The other signals we began to notice in Lindsay were loss of weight, loss of appetite, frequent complaints of an upset stomach, and inability to eat whole meals. Her inability to complete a meal was probably the result of ingesting large quantities of hydrocodone or other opiates before she advanced to heroin. We noticed mood swings, irritability, and defensiveness became more and more common. Other warning signs you might observe are acne or sores on their face or hair picked off of their hands. Heroin causes a histamine release making the skin feel itchy.

Lindsay's most extensive symptom was isolation. There would be long periods of time where we did not know where she was or if she was alive. When we would attempt to contact her, calls and texts were not returned. During the time she was living at home, she would isolate herself by staying in her room and not engaging with us as a family.

As time went on other indications appeared. One particular day, I noticed spoons had been disappearing from our flatware drawer. I mentioned the disappearing spoons to my husband. I would find spoons burnt on the bottom in a bedside nightstand or in her purse or car. Cotton swabs also began disappearing. I would find the small cotton from swabs on the bathroom sink and floor. Later, I learned addicts will remove the cotton from the cotton swabs to use as a filter when drawing up heroin into a syringe. Alongside the cotton from the swab, I would find a bottle of water opened in the bathroom with only a small portion of the water gone from the bottle. Bottled water can be used to mix heroin and the cap can be used for heating. Heroin can also be smuggled into the home using the cap from the bottled water. Let me explain; Heroin is usually in a small baggie. An addict informed me he would sneak heroin into his home by gluing the small bag of heroin to the inside of the cap of bottled water. His parents never thought to check his bottle of water for heroin. I have heard water from the toilet tank can be used to mix heroin as well.

Aluminum foil was another item missing. Instead of finding the foil in its designated spot in the kitchen, I would find it under the guest bathroom sink. I learned foil can be used to heat the heroin to the point of boiling and the vapor can be inhaled or the powder snorted with the help of some type of tube (possibly a hollowed out pen, so be on the lookout for pens without the ink). Look for any type of unusual homemade tube in which your child can inhale or snort opiates or heroin, such as straws (specifically cut in half) or a toilet roll tube. Addicts will use shorter tubes to inhale the fumes because they don't want smoke to stick to the tube and result in a loss of the drug. Along with the aluminum foil I found countless lighters. Some parents say they observed missing candles. If you are missing candles or finding an overabundance of lighters, this may be an indication your child is abusing drugs. I spotted burns on the dresser in the guest bedroom, along with doilies that had burn marks. I then began to find needles in drawers and under mattresses.

Look for tourniquets and be aware they can come in many forms. You might find rubber bands, shoelaces, purse straps, belts, or even tie backs from your drapes. For example, my husband and I came home from church one Sunday and found a tie of his in the family room. He had not worn the tie, much less thrown the tie on the family room floor. In another instance, I had packed a box for Goodwill which contained some drapes I was donating. I came home one day to find the box opened and one of the tie backs on the floor next to a family room chair. The tight band of a tourniquet is used to cut off blood flow, much like if you were having blood drawn. The vein engorges and you are able to stick the needle into the vessel. I learned to look for anything out of the ordinary that could possibly be used as a homemade tourniquet.

Other signs you may observe:
*Twitching while they sleep
*Rolled up dollar bills or cards (snorting)
*Small plastic bags or balloons (heroin storage)
*Razor blades, IDs, or credit cards with residue
*Nasal spray bottles (used for snorting the heroin & water mixture)

Someone addicted to drugs will have their paraphernalia on their person (e.g.: inside a pocket, taped to their leg, or hidden under their breast) or in close proximity. Check purses, pockets, backpacks, cars, behind mirrors, under dressers, between mattresses, behind their cell phone battery, inside socks, cigarette boxes, Altoid tins, and in toilet tanks.

Lesson: Look everywhere. If they are using and you are looking, you will find the evidence.

Confront
The Nathan Approach

One of the hardest lessons learned as the mom of an addict was figuring out the best way to confront my adult child when I knew she was continuing to abuse drugs. My daughter would lie, manipulate, and become agitated when I confronted her with signs of usage. I learned, over a period of time, her defensiveness and denial were all part of her manipulation. At first, in the early days of dealing with her, I often backed down because her excuses seemed plausible. When she dozed and nodded off: "I'm really tired today. Work was exhausting." When her color was more pale than normal: "I bought a lighter shade of make-up." When my daughter was constantly sniffing: "I'm sick, that's why my nose is running" (This is a sign of histamine release). When she would sweat profusely she would say: "I've been sick, my temperature must be breaking, and that's why I'm sweating" (This is a sign of withdrawal).

As I began to school myself regarding addiction, I wanted to know more about how to confront an addict, since this was my biggest weakness. Some suggested not being unnecessarily confrontational because the situation could escalate to dangerous levels, especially if the person was under the influence. Using statements such as, "You are high" and "Where did all the money go," is considered direct and ineffective.

When I finally decided to confront Lindsay in another way besides my emotional outbursts, there seemed to be a lack of satisfactory guidance, in my opinion, at the time, in how to best confront her on my own as a parent (Many parents will attempt to confront their child on their own initially, mostly because parents are either unaware of parent addiction coaching and intervention assistance, or because a parent may think if an interventionist is used the situation may worsen. At first, these were my thoughts). So I developed a model of my own on confronting. I took the prototype from the story in the Bible where Nathan confronts King David about his adultery with Bathsheba. Even though this passage found in 2 Samuel 12:1-15 involves confronting King David's adulterous affair, I found Nathan's approach was quite helpful in how I could approach Lindsay's drug usage.

I learned I might be able to help my child get her life back by taking the painful steps of approaching her addiction in a different manner besides emotional manipulation. I would like to take you through eight steps I have found useful in confronting my addict child, using what I call the Nathan Approach. This will require you to read the story. Do not worry, the story is not long, but it is full of rich lessons on how to handle confronting. Read the story: 2 Samuel 12:1-15 and let's walk through the Nathan Approach Model. As you read the passage, ask yourself what methods Nathan used to confront King David.

The LORD sent Nathan to David. When he came to him, he said, "There were two men in a certain town, one rich and the other poor. The rich man had a very large number of sheep and cattle, but the poor man had nothing except one little ewe lamb he had bought. He raised it, and it grew up with him and his children. It shared his food, drank from his cup and even slept in his arms. It was like a daughter to him.

"Now a traveler came to the rich man, but the rich man refrained from taking one of his own sheep or cattle to prepare a meal for the traveler who had come to him. Instead, he took the ewe lamb that belonged to the poor man and prepared it for the one who had come to him."

David burned with anger against the man and said to Nathan, "As surely as the LORD lives, the man who did this must die! He must pay for that lamb four times over, because he did such a thing and had no pity."

Then Nathan said to David, "You are the man! This is what the LORD, the God of Israel, says: 'I anointed you king over Israel, and I delivered you from the hand of Saul. I gave your master's house to you, and your master's wives into your arms. I gave you all Israel and Judah. And if all this had been too little, I would have given you even more. Why did you despise the word of the LORD by doing what is evil in his eyes? You struck down Uriah the Hittite with the sword and took his wife to be your own. You killed him with the sword of the Ammonites. Now, therefore, the sword will never depart from your house, because you despised me and took the wife of Uriah the Hittite to be your own.'

"This is what the LORD says: 'Out of your own household I am going to bring calamity on you. Before your very eyes I will take your wives and give them to one who is close to you, and he will sleep with your wives in broad daylight. You did it in secret, but I will do this thing in broad daylight before all Israel.'"

Then David said to Nathan, "I have sinned against the LORD."

Nathan replied, "The LORD has taken away your sin. You are not going to die. But because by doing this you have shown utter contempt for the LORD, the son born to you will die."

After Nathan had gone home, the LORD struck the child that Uriah's wife had borne to David, and he became ill.

Did you catch the approach Nathan used to confront David? Emotional manipulation? Anger? Yelling? Threatening? Passivity? Avoidance? Dismissal? No! Out of our own frustrations we often resort to such means because we do not know how to deal with the circumstance. If these are not the most beneficial ways to confront, then how do you deal with approaching your adult addict child? I think Nathan's model of confronting can give us insight into dealing with your adult child addict.

8 STEPS WE CAN LEARN FROM THE TEXT

1. The Lord sent Nathan.

Your approach: Go in the strength of God, not your own strength. By God sending Nathan, we can deduce He knew about King David's secret. God knows the circumstance of our child's addiction. As you go in God's strength, ask him for the same wisdom he gave Nathan. Ask God to allow you to see what He sees. Ask God to give you a heart like His. Ask God to remove any pride in your own heart. Know God walks with you.

2. Nathan goes with a story given to him by God.

Your approach: Be prepared in what you will say. Ask God to show you what words to use. Nathan does not put David on the defense, or approach him with harsh words. He approaches him respectfully and finds something David can relate to like his abundance of sheep. Choose your words wisely. Approach your loved one with respect. Talk to her. Do not talk at her. Dialogue with your child. If need be, write down what you will say.

3. Nathan exposes the secret.

Your approach: Expose the secret with facts and evidence like finding paraphernalia, or noticing physical, emotional, social, and mental changes. Take out the emotion, use evidence and facts. For example: "I found these burned spoons in your room with cotton swabs. You say you are not using, but here is the evidence that says you are." Maybe it is more subtle: They are staying up days on end, and then sleep for days. They avoid eye contact or isolate themselves; their color is ashen or they have lost a significant amount of weight. Do not use emotional manipulation, threatening, crying, yelling, or anger. Go with a motive of restoration. Have your antennas up if you suspect drug abuse. If they are using, you will find the evidence. He will display physical, mental, and emotional symptoms eventually. The drug will wear on him.

4. The problem is not between Nathan and King David.

Your approach: Don't make it a personal issue. No matter how much the addict blame shifts, guilt's, manipulates, or attacks you, the problem is not you personally. Keep the focus on evidence of usage.

5. God did not tell Nathan how King David would respond.

Your approach: Brace yourself for any reaction, especially defensiveness and anger. Most addicts will lie when confronted. When there is evidence, they will try to explain it away, or react by becoming very angry and walk off. Notice King David was "furious" when first confronted.

Don't let anger deter you, but also notice something else. When Nathan says to David, "You are that man," David quickly realizes he has been exposed; his secret out in the open. What is strikingly beautiful is David's response to his secret: He acknowledges his sin. He acknowledges what he has done. God already knew his secret, and God knows the secret of the addicts using, even when they continue to deny or lie. Ideally, an addict may have the same response David had: open acknowledgement.

6. Nathan speaks the truth in love to King David.

Your approach: Reflect God's heart. Speak truth in love. Stay focused on facts. Resist speaking with venom. Always check your motive before confronting. There is a way to be firm and not buckle under emotion. Remove the emotion and dialogue. Talk to the child, not the addict in your child (Sandy Swenson).

7. When confronted King David confesses.

Your approach: Realize a confession may come, or it may not. If a confession does come, acknowledge your child for being honest. Admitting their addiction or drug abuse is tremendous headway. However, most will fight the truth and fight to keep the secret.

As an example to confessing the use of drugs and having a problem with addiction, I recently received a comment on a blog post. The comment brought tears to my eyes:

"I begged him not to put that needle in his arm. Very compassionately, he came to me pulled me close to him and told me words I will never forget. "If I do this the pain will stop, if I don't I will be in pain and I will stay in pain until I do it again."

Addicts are in a lot of pain. The drug has them in a vicious cycle where they often see no hope of coming out or ever being free from the drug. Offer your child hope and unconditional love while still maintaining your boundaries.

8. King David faced consequences for his actions, but God was still merciful.

Your approach: Extend mercy, but have consequences. For example, you may set the rule there is to be no usage if a child is living in your home. If your child relapses, the consequence could be detox, inpatient rehab, and a recovery plan for the next year. Think through the consequences you will implement. You will have to set what the boundaries are and STICK TO THEM! Always remember the end goal is restoration. This is where a parent addiction coach can help you write a recovery plan.

As you begin to work through the Nathan Approach, there are a few things to consider. Do not presume to implement the model perfectly the first time. Keep trying, allowing yourself to learn the concepts of confronting. Do not expect too much too soon. As parents of addicts, we have unknown habits we have developed in how we react to our addict child, usually tied to their manipulation. The habits are also tied to how we perceive our child in our mind, often picturing them as adolescents instead of grown adults. One suggestion is to consider a third party with a coaching session or counselor who can mediate when confronting, similar to an intervention. This changes the dynamic of the situation because the parent and the child are not alone, thus the addict is not able to manipulate the parent. Learning to change your behavior and your reaction to your child will come with time and practice. Maybe this analogy will help you understand how to change your habits in dealing or confronting your adult addict child:

Autobiography in Five Short Chapters (Portia Nelson)

I

I walk, down the street.

There is a deep hole in the sidewalk.

I fall in

I am lost ... I am helpless

It isn't my fault.

It takes forever to find a way out.

II

I walk down the same street.

There is a deep hole in the sidewalk.

I pretend I don't see it.

I fall in again.

I can't believe I am in the same place.

But, it isn't my fault.

It still takes a long time to get out.

III

I walk down the same street.

There is a deep hole in the sidewalk.

I see it is there.

I still fall in ... it's a habit.

My eyes are open.

I know where I am.

It is my fault.

I get out immediately.

IV

I walk down the same street.

There is a deep hole in the sidewalk.

I walk around it.

V

I walk down another street.

Before you confront your addicted child, know when and how you will implement the confrontation, and have a treatment plan in place.

"Have a treatment program already picked out. Stay in contact with that facility occasionally to verify availability, costs and admission procedures. When the addict asks for help, you want to take advantage of the window of opportunity. In the meantime, take good care of yourself so you can offer healthy assistance when your loved one or friend asks for help." Mike Speakman

There is an absolutely fascinating redemptive end to King David's story. You can find the story in Psalm 51. As King David was restored to wholeness after being confronted by Nathan, I pray your loved one could find the same restoration and redemption.

Have a Plan for Help

Figuring out what to do next to get help for our daughter Lindsay was filled with a mass of confusion. Like many of you, my husband and I had questions: "How do we find help? Where do we go to obtain assistance? What are the next steps?"

We learned the process as we stumbled our way through: Detox was her immediate need. Lindsay's second need was some type of rehab or recovery inpatient residential assistance. Thirdly, a quality treatment plan was essential. We had to be able to afford treatment without being ruined financially. A plan was also needed for Lindsay's to transition back into society once she completed the program. Lindsay had no insurance coverage. Most substance abusers are in a similar situation, they have no insurance. Some adult addicts are fortunate and can be covered by a parent's insurance policy. As you may already know, addiction treatment can be very expensive.

I have read where some parents are able to pay privately, but for most, the care is too expensive. If you are fortunate enough to have insurance which covers your child, review your plan and research centers which offer detox and inpatient rehab or recovery. From experience, 30, 60, or 90 days is not enough time for an addict to recover. If your insurance covers an inpatient year long program, consider this option other than the shorter treatment period.

For parents with no money and no assets, there are programs out there which are free or low cost. The first time Lindsay asked for help she detoxed at home and was admitted to a Teen Challenge Program. (I would advise against allowing your adult addict child to detox at home, it is emotionally heart wrenching to watch). Teen Challenge worked with us on financing and we paid monthly payments which were affordable. Another time my daughter relapsed she detoxed at a non-medical women's facility called The Healing Place. The cost was $0. Once her detox stay was completed she immediately entered a yearlong inpatient residential sober facility called St. Jude's for Women in Louisville. The program was very low cost plus she received excellent care. There were phases Lindsay, as a resident, had to work through. Eventually, my daughter held a job and began to get her life back.

Most recently when Lindsay relapsed, she was able to be admitted to a medical detox center for 30 days called Jefferson Alcohol and Drug Abuse Center (JADAC). The cost was only $50. While she was at JADAC Lindsay was assigned a counselor and a case worker which developed a plan of care for her specific needs. The caseworker and my daughter worked together on a long term plan which would begin when she completed detox. The counselor kept us informed on the options available once Lindsay was released, but in the end, the decision was Lindsay's. She could walk free once she detoxed or she could continue a plan of recovery. Lindsay decided to enter a sober living facility.

Where Can You Go For Help?

I do not know who you are, your circumstance, or where you live, but if you are searching for assistance I hope this fabulous resource will help: *Free Rehab Centers* (Listed on the Resource page of the book under Treatment Locators and Help section). Many of these options are low cost or offer free assistance for your child.

If you are not already a member of *The Addicts Mom*, consider joining. The site group is for moms; however fathers have been known to join too. They have a resource link on their page with various free or low cost rehabs in various states. Also, review the excellent *Help Guide* at the end of the book under the Treatment Locators and Help section. The *Help Guide* will assist in what you should consider when choosing a treatment center.

What Do I Do If They Refuse Treatment?

On another note, let's say you have confronted your adult child addict and they respond in anger and denial. If your child is living at home with you, consider purchasing a drug screening test from a local store such as Walmart or Walgreens. Randomly sample their urine to check for drugs in their system. If your child is using he will most likely become angry and refuse a urine drug screening test (What is your plan if they refuse a screening test?). My suggestion would be have a list of detox resources in your area and treatment facilities/sober houses and offer them help to find treatment. Spell out your consequences clearly to your child. Once, when Lindsay refused treatment, my husband and I wrote her a letter, informed her she could no longer live with us, and we gave her a resource list she could call of options for treatment. We told Lindsay we loved her, and to contact us when she was ready for help. Lindsay left, but within a few weeks, she appeared at our door stating she was ready to go to treatment.

If your adult child concurs to the urine test, be sure to turn off the water faucet valve in the bathroom and place blue colored dye in the toilet so they cannot dilute the specimen with tap or toilet water. Also, stand in the bathroom with your child while they urinate in the cup.

I have heard of bizarre tactics addicts will use to falsify specimen results. In one instance, I heard of an addict taping a tube to their leg with an attached cup of someone else's clean urine. While they pretended to be urinating, a small bulb was manipulated to stream the urine into the cup. Crazy? Yes. My point: Know there are tricks to passing the urine test. Another tidbit: Buy a kit with a measurement for normal urine temperature to guard against the most common trick of diluting the urine with water. The question for you as a parent of an addict: if the drug screen is positive, what will be your plan of action?

Consider filing a petition for a court ordered intervention. There are states which advocate for legal interventions to reduce mortalities from drug overdoses. The state, in which I live, Kentucky, has such an intervention called Casey's Law (KY & OH). The law is for involuntary treatment and provides a way of intervening for someone who is unable to recognize his or her need for treatment due to their impairment from the drugs. The law allows parents, relatives, or friends to petition the court on behalf of the person who is a substance abuser. If you live in Kentucky you will need Form 700A to complete and file in your city.

An acquaintance of mine, who is an addict's mother, Kimberly Wright, is a leader for the Kentucky State Chapter of *The Addicts Mom* Facebook group. She has further insight from her experience filing Casey's Law for her adult addict daughter and the steps she walked through in the process. Here is her advice:

1. Have your two assessment appointments which are required for Casey's Law already scheduled before you file the petition. One assessment has to be performed by a physician; the other assessment needs to be by another qualified healthcare professional such as a therapist or counselor.

2. Try to schedule the two assessments close together so the judge will have the assessments for the hearing. It is your responsibility to get your child to the assessment appointments.

Let the judge's clerk know dates for scheduled assessment appointments. When the petition has been filed, your child will be served with papers by mail. The sheriff will inform your child they are court ordered to be assessed.

3. Also, you are to hand deliver a copy to your child of the court's order for the two assessments to be done. Advice: take a witness with you and ask them to accompany you to court so the witness can testify they saw you hand your child the court papers. If your child does not show up to court as ordered a warrant will be issued for their arrest for contempt of court.

4. Have a recovery plan in place before the court date. Where will they detox and receive treatment? You are responsible for setting up their recovery plan and paying for the cost of treatment.

5. Be prepared for your child to be really mad. They may threaten to run and say they will refuse to comply. "You are trying to put me in jail," (or other guilt and blame shifting statements).

6. Your child can ask for another hearing and a second opinion.

7. The judge will order what is recommended according to the assessment findings. So if your child tries to negotiate an outpatient treatment plan, the judge will go with what is recommended by the two professionals. The decision will also depend upon how much they are using.

8. The papers you file will ask you why you feel the court should order treatment, or why you think they are in danger to you or to themselves. Write down everything you know and have seen from your child's addiction.

Another example similar to Casey's Law is The Jennifer Act, (IN & FL). Wherever you are on this journey with your addicted child, whether just beginning to walk the road of addiction or being a seasoned sojourner, if you have not already done so, research your options. Resources are out there and help is available.

Receive Training in CPR/Carry Naloxone

If I had not known CPR on the Saturday night Lindsay overdosed, I believe she would not be with us today. I taught CPR for years, so when I saw Lindsay's cyanotic lips, agonal breathing, and ashen color, I immediately went into nurse mode. When EMS got lost on the way to our house, I really did not think my daughter would ever wake up, or worse, she would go into full cardiac arrest. Those 30 minutes seemed like an eternity.

I also attribute her recovery to my son Gabriel, who acted quickly and alerted us to her overdose. Most interestingly, the day before Lindsay overdosed Gabriel asked me what to do if someone overdosed. I told him not to run, but to call 911. Then, I walked him through a mini CPR course, emphasizing the biggest concern was time, an open airway, and oxygen. I explained to Gabriel what happens to the brain when deprived of oxygen, even for a short period. After only one minute, brain cells begin to die, although survival is still possible without neurological deficits. At the three minute mark, serious brain damage is likely, and at ten minutes without breathing, most brain cells have died and the person normally has irreversible damage with an unlikely recovery. Fifteen minutes marks a virtually impossible recovery. The only exception would be if someone were very cold, such as being submerged in extremely frigid water.

The night Lindsay overdosed, Gabriel found her slumped over at the computer desk. He told me she was blue and not breathing. He should have probably moved her to the floor because it is a flat surface, but instead he opened her airway while she was still in the computer chair. Gabriel said when he opened her airway Lindsay took a big gasping breath. From there, he ran to our bedroom to awaken us. All in all, one minute may have passed from the time Gabriel found her, ran up two flights of stairs, and ran back down those same stairs. He was working quickly, just like I had instructed him to do in an emergency.

As a parent of an addict you are at a high risk of possibly finding your child from an overdose. If you are not already trained in CPR consider making this a priority for you to become trained. Every major city has CPR through the American Heart Association or through the Red Cross.

And about Naloxone? Keep it with your lipstick.

What Should I Not Do?

Part Two

Deny, Be Passive, or Emotionally Manipulate Your Child

Denial is huge in parents of addicts. Denial is an obstacle to getting much needed assistance and treatment. As I shared earlier, my husband and I rationalized, justified, and explained away our daughter's phase: "All teens and young adults experience." According to Merriam-Webster denial is *"a psychological defense mechanism in which confrontation with a personal problem or with reality is avoided by denying the existence of the problem or reality."*

The actual word's origin and history means *"unconscious suppression of painful or embarrassing feelings."* Ignoring the signs of addiction can be easy. It is a result of our defense mechanism kicking in and leaving us in a state of unbelief, even if the evidence is right under our nose.

What I failed to realize in the beginning, was how my denial was hurting my child. If you have suspicions your child is using, your suspicions are probably correct. Instead of denying their involvement with drugs, investigate further. Hopefully, they are not using, but if they are and you start looking you will find the evidence. Do not down play your suspicions or the seriousness of substance abuse. Trust your instincts. It is much better to be wrong than to miss the signs your child may need help with a substance abuse problem or addiction.

Passivity or emotional manipulation is also a mistake to avoid when approaching an addict. I did this. I was unsure of what the next step was or how to handle the discovery of Lindsay's usage. Sometimes I ignored the signs and said nothing, hoping Lindsay would come to her senses and stop. Sometimes I confronted her in anger with yelling and screaming. I belittled. I threatened. I cried. I begged. I shamed. Every emotion I spilled out.

When I look back, I realize the crux of my emotional manipulation was fear. I did not look at my tears or my screaming outbursts as manipulation at the time. I was just so afraid my child was going to die. The fear was relentless. My stomach was constantly in knots, and my thoughts were consumed with the nightmare my child may die in her addiction. When Lindsay went to treatment and then relapsed several times, I had to come to grips with my fear. I began to turn from fear to faith. I had to trust my faith would be stronger than my fear. My faith was not in God keeping Lindsay from dying, but in knowing God was bigger than her addiction.

I had to ask myself, "Could I still maintain my belief in a God whose Word claims He is good, if my daughter died in her addiction? Would God still be a good God?" God's Word states He is good, and since God will not be contrary to His Word, then I deduced that God would still be a good God. The situation was not good; however, I discovered God is not defined by my circumstance or my emotions. Jesus Christ still died and was resurrected. The story of the cross and redemption did not change because my daughter was an addict, nor will it change if she dies in her addiction.

Be Deceived, Blame Shift, Or Take on Guilt

As you may have already unearthed there are certain behaviors your child will display, such as statements of guilt, deception, and manipulation. The addict in your child will become angry with you and even "hate you" when their coveted addiction is threatened. These behaviors are universal to addicts. Detaching the addict from your child is essential when understanding their irrational thinking patterns. Sandy Swenson, a mother of an addict says this:

My son and the addict may share the same shadow but they will not share my love. My son is the one I want to see live beyond tomorrow. Once I stopped caring if the addict hated me, the addict hated me even more. He didn't like the word "No." He yelled and cursed and threatened, viciously pulling on heartstrings and fears, trying to trick me into betraying my son. But I didn't. My love is a rock solid foundation for my son to stand on (or take his next step), not the addict. And now they both know it. Eventually the manipulative gyrations completely stopped, but that's not the end of the story.

"Hi mom. I was thinking of you and just wanna say "I love you." I feel like I'm missing out on my amazing mom because I don't call very often. Hug toss."

You may initially believe some of the lies from your adult addict child, because they seem plausible, or you may be to the point of frustration because of the manipulation and lies. Remember the addiction is speaking rather than the child. For starters, train yourself to recognize statements of deception, guilt, and blame shifting comments. Remove the emotional aspect or the urge you feel to scream or yell when you discover they have lied, are manipulating, or blaming you for their problems. If your child is irrational have a boundary set and a plan of how you handle the lies without manipulating your child. Understand "addiction lives in the lie." Libby Cataldi, Author of *Stay Close*, and the mother of an adult addict:

"Addiction is based in silence-don't talk, don't feel, don't trust, don't share, don't question, don't let anybody know. Addiction can only exist in the lie- if the addict keeps the lie- he keeps the addiction. Addiction does its best work in the shadows."

Deception comes in other forms such as parents thinking all their child needs is detox and the problem of their drug use will be fixed. I remember thinking the first time Lindsay went to detox and recovery: "What a relief, when she completes this, we can all move on and addiction will be behind us." The deceptive thinking was out of my ignorance. I really did not have a clue about addiction and the battle we are still fighting today.

Remember, detox is NOT recovery. Your addict child may have gone through the physical withdrawals; however there are emotional and spiritual components to work through. Also, your child's brain has been affected physiologically by drugs. Addiction is not an issue of morals; it is an issue with predispositions to its effects on the physiological make-up of an individual. Whether you believe addiction is a disease, a matter of choice, or self-medicating, drugs do affect your brain and have lasting physical implications. Substance abuse researcher, A. Thomas McLellan, Ph.D., CEO and Co-Founder Treatment Research Institute, lost a son to addiction; he wrote an article for Huff Post Healthy Living and says this:

"...Something happens in the brains of about 10 percent of those who use -- we don't yet know exactly all that happens in those brains but for sure there is triggering of genetic expression, and likely induction of immunologic reactions. We know that those biological changes have primary effects in the brain especially in the areas responsible for governing judgment, inhibition, motivation and

learning. We do not yet know why some drugs produce these effects in some people; how much or often one has to use to bring about these changes, or how long these brain changes last. And we do not yet know which of those who drink or use for the first time will go on to become addicted. But we do know two things for sure. Nobody -- nobody -- has their first drink in order to become an addict. And we know for sure that the brains of those who become addicted are very different from the brains they started out with."

Be aware of your own deceptive thinking. For instance just because I claim to be a follower of Christ, and have prayed to God to not let my daughter die, does not mean she will not die from the consequences of her addiction. However, do not be deceived into thinking there is no hope, your child is too far gone, or they have reached a point of no return. As long as God gives breath, freedom from addiction is possible.

It is not uncommon for parents to blame friends, school, a crisis event, or to blame each other for their addict child's usage. Vivian Hyatt writes a great example of blame shifting and guilt in The Gospel Coalition Blog entitled *Taking Comfort in Cain*:

"Did Adam and Eve blame their parenting? Did they lie awake, nights, staring into the blackness, tracing every detail of Cain's upbringing? Did we spank enough? Teach enough? Play enough? Pray enough? Is it ever enough? This one always tested the limits. He just wanted to get by, play this charade of obedience, but his heart wasn't in it. We should have recognized it. Eve, you should have! You tested the limits yourself! Whoa, wait a minute, Adam! You flat-out disobeyed! Besides, he's the son most like you. Out in the fields with you, learning the trade. Did you ever talk about things? Did you think he'd just figure it out on his own? Did you tell him you hid from God once? Cringed when he called your name? Did you warn him of the consequences of going his own way? Well, did you?"

Vivian Hyatt's words are a perfect example of how parents and addicts play the blame game. Blaming accomplishes nothing, it only fuels a high velocity of emotions to erupt and keeps the focus off the actions of drug abuse and shifts the focus to your reaction. Parents of addicts often feel tremendous guilt, blaming themselves for their child's addiction.

As Al-anon teaches: You did not cause your child's addiction. You yourself cannot cure your child's addiction. You cannot control your child's addiction.

Sandy Swenson says:

"I did not cause my son to become an addict. As a parent, I do not possess that power. Addiction happens because a renegade sip or snort or sniff crosses an invisible line between want and need."

Lesson: Stop playing the blame game. You did not cause their addiction.

Enable

No one wants to wear the label of an enabler. Seriously, who wants to have this label plastered on the front of their chest? An enabler often thinks he is helping his loved one, but instead is enabling him to continue in addiction. The two are distinctly different. When first dealing with my daughter, I did not fully understand enabling.

For years my husband and I rescued Lindsay, bailing her out of situation after situation, thinking we were helping, hoping each time she would come to her senses. We enabled out of fear and guilt. What if she died on the streets? How could we let that happen? We often paid her rent, put gas in her car, bought groceries, purchased clothes, paid cell phone bills, and handed her money. Her father bought her cars, tires, and paid her car insurance. We thought we were helping her, but what we were actually doing was spoon feeding Lindsay's addiction. We were paying her expenses, and her money was going to drugs. It wasn't until we stopped rescuing her and accepted she would have to face her own consequences. As parents, we realized death was a possible consequence of her addiction; however, she was more likely to live once we stopped enabling.

UNDERSTANDING THE LABEL

"Helping is doing something for someone that they are not

capable of doing themselves. Enabling is doing for someone things that they could, and should be doing themselves." Games Alcoholics Play.

Do you understand the idea of enabling? Enabling is when you make it easy for your child to continue in their substance abuse. If you are unsure if you are enabling or helping, maybe the enabling checklist below will help you identify unhealthy tendencies. The enabling checklist is from one of the PAL Group lessons provided by Mike Speakman.

ENABLING CHECKLIST
(used with permission)

Check off the ones which you would answer "Yes."

- o Have you ever covered a financial debt that is the result of behavioral dysfunction or drug/alcohol related?
- o Have you ever made a call to cancel an appointment on the person's behalf due to dysfunctional behavior?
- o Have you ever "called in sick" or made excuses to his or her job or school?
- o Have you ever not called the police after the person was physically abusive?
- o Have you ever let the person come and live with you because he or she has run out of money?
- o As a result of repeatedly running out of money, have you continued to loan the person money?
- o Have you ever bailed the person out of jail for an arrest connected with drugs and/or physical abuse?
- o Have you ever excused the person from keeping a commitment because he/she is "depressed"?
- o Are you afraid to confront the person about their behaviors for fear of violence?
- o Are you afraid to confront the person about their behaviors for fear they will leave you?
- o Do you sometimes believe their behaviors are not so bad because "they are only occurring in the home"?
- o Do you sometimes act is if you believe the person's excuses

even when you know he/she is lying?

- o Do you sometimes think it is because of you the person behaved the way they did?
- o Do you prefer not to talk to anyone about the problem because you're ashamed?
- o Do you allow the person to come back to the house even after he or she has been physically destructive?
- o Do you make excuses to your children for the person's behaviors?
- o Do you threaten to leave the relationship, and then not follow through on leaving?
- o Do you pretend the chemically dependent is sick when they are really coming off a binge?
- o Have you ever taken drugs with the chemically dependent so you can be together?
- o Have you ever obtained drugs for the chemically dependent?

If you checked off three or more of these questions, you have probably been enabling someone.

SHEDDING THE LABEL

After reviewing the above checklist, I hope the following steps will help you start shedding the label of enabler. They are by no means all inclusive of halting your enabling traits, and you may even reflect on your own pattern of enabling and devise a plan of your own. Consider these concepts on enabling according to *Games Alcoholics Play*:

How to Stop Enabling

- Cease doing anything that allows the addict to continue their current lifestyle.
- Do nothing to "help" the addict that he could or would be doing himself if he were not drinking.
- Stop lying, covering up, or making excuses for the addict.
- Do not take on responsibilities or duties that rightfully belong to the addict.
- Do not give or loan the addict money.

- Don't 'rescue' the addict by bailing him out of jail or paying his fines.
- Do not scold, argue or plead with the addict.
- Do not react to his latest misadventures, so that he can respond to your reaction rather than his actions.
- Do not try to drink with the alcoholic addict.
- Set boundaries and stick to them. Don't make threats.
- Carefully explain to the addict the boundaries you have set, and explain the boundaries are for you, not for him.

In addition to learning about enabling and setting boundaries, I learned about the issue of delayed emotional growth. Mike Speakman defines delayed emotional growth this way:

"A dysfunctional condition experienced by a child who has matured physically and intellectually but not psychologically, and has difficulty coping with the normal stresses and responsibilities of adulthood."

As you read the following six steps, ask yourself: "How do I see my adult child? Do I still view him or her as an adolescent or younger child?" When I asked myself these questions, I realized I had been looking at Lindsay like she was a sixteen year old girl, and she is twenty-nine. All this time I was reacting to her and dealing with her as a teenager. I am slowing learning to treat her as an adult as I repeatedly review these six steps.

6 STEPS FOR HELPING YOUR ADDICTED ADULT CHILD
by Mike Speakman (used with permission)

Step 1: Learn about your adult child's problem of delayed emotional growth.

In addition to alcohol or drug abuse, your child may have another issue. It serves as a silent partner in keeping addiction active and resistant to change, but can be quite difficult to identify. Simply, delayed emotional growth means that you still see your adult child as an adolescent or younger child. He or she is an adult now and deserves to be treated like one.

Step 2: Transition to an adult-to-adult relationship.

In American culture, there is no formal rite of passage when a child becomes an adult. Key to helping your adult child mature emotionally is for everyone to acknowledge that he or she is now an adult. It will also mean treating your adult child like an adult, especially in difficult situations. Even though it was not your fault, you may choose to apologize to your adult child for having treated her as an adolescent for too long.

Step 3: Set realistic boundaries and consequences for your adult child.

Once your adult-to-adult relationship is in place, you can establish what is acceptable and what happens when those mutually agreed upon boundaries are crossed. When over-stepping bounds, your child has to handle the consequences as an adult. You no longer will over help him and you both know why. Your communication is now easier, because you are dealing with an adult. It will take time and practice to learn, but you will see the wisdom in treating your son or daughter as an adult, even when they act like a child. Your adult child may need to adjust to this new perspective, but having an understanding of what is acceptable and what happens when that agreement isn't respected helps you - and your adult child - stay on course.

Step 4: Cut strings to help your adult child become more responsible.

Strings are always financial. Most are obvious, but often they're not. You'll be able to pinpoint certain situations where strings are keeping your adult child from making positive changes. Once you learn to identify these strings, you can plan the safest way to cut them.

Step 5: Write your own plan for helping your adult child.

Written plans provide road maps for achievement as well as accountability. A Parents Plan can be created by you with or without the help of a professional. As parents, it's important to agree with each other about what you will and will not do to help your loved one. It's recommended that you complete the plan before approaching your adult child.

Step 6: Help your adult child write their own plan for moving forward in life.

Your adult child might also want to have a Recovering Person Plan, which lists goals such as finding a job, saving money, paying debts, steps for "cutting strings," and consequences of relapse. A professional can best help your adult child create this plan. And, even though the goals need to come from your loved one, you have a say about his goals when he requires your assistance as his parents.

PUTTING ON THE LABEL OF CHRIST

Putting on the new and shedding the old is a day to day process of dying to self and living to Christ. Colossians 3:10 tells us to: *"Put on your new nature, and be renewed as you learn to know your Creator and become like him"* (NLT). Shedding the label of an enabler may be tough. That is not to say you cannot begin to change today. As you focus more on your relationship with Christ, draw near to Him, and nurture your relationship with Him, you will find strength for the road and hope for tomorrow. May your faith prompt you to let your identity (and label) be in Christ.

Extra Resource:

A Letter to My Family

As I mention early on in the book I am a member of *The Addicts Mom*, a support group for mothers who have adult children who struggle with addiction. Resources regarding addiction abound in the group, so it is not unusual for mom's to post the latest news on drug intervention laws, information about support meetings in your area, where to find free or low cost treatment for your child, or any number of things having to do with being a parent of an addict. While browsing my Facebook feed I came across this letter posted by Kimberly Wright, Administrator TAM Kentucky Chapter. The author is unknown, so I am unable to give credit.

I decided to include the letter in the book because it gives deep insight in understanding your child's thinking and addiction from their view, not from your view. Pay special attention and see if you are able to identify statements of guilt, hints of delayed emotional growth, blame-shifting, justification, rationalization, excuses and accusatory remarks. Look for the way the author denies and avoids responsibility and ways he is manipulating you, the parent, to feel guilty. By glimpsing into the addict's mind, hopefully the message will help you to have a better understanding of their struggle. The letter is unedited, with the exception of dividing the letter into paragraphs:

I want to introduce myself to you; I'm your qualifier and the reason you're here. You believe just because you gave me life and raised me that you know me, but you really don't. I'd like to use this time to introduce the real me to you so maybe you can gain a better understanding of why I am the way I am, why I do the things I do and why I've done some of the things I've done. I don't know if I was born an addict but I do know the first time I got high an addict was born.

First of all, you have to accept the fact that I think differently than you do. Some of this will make sense to you and some of this will sound like excuses that you've heard before, but just know that the ones that sound like excuses are based on my fact, my perspective, and the knowledge and experience of the people who are trying to help me get clean. These are people I have placed my trust and faith in because all they want from me is to succeed in my endeavor to stay clean for another day.

You have your own goals for me like going to college, getting a job, getting married and finally having kids so you can have grandkids and can show all of your friends their pictures. See these are your goals for me and not necessarily my goals for myself.

Let me try to explain how I see things. See, you think I have a drug problem but I don't; I have a living problem. You think I use drugs but the reality is that drugs use me. Drugs are for those of us that can't handle reality, and reality is for people like you that can't handle their drugs. To me, reality is a nice place to visit but I really don't like living there. I live in constant fear of letting you down; of not living up to your expectations. I put off doing things out of fear and you call me a procrastinator, but procrastination is just a 5 syllable word for fear.

Drugs make me feel alive and normal, but they also make me paranoid, incoherent and both destructive and pathetically and relentlessly self-destructive. Then I would do unconscionable things in order to feel normal and alive again. Drugs gave me wings and then slowly took away my sky. I looked to drugs for courage and they made me a coward. You say that I had always been a sensitive, perceptive, joyful and exceptionally bright child, but on drugs I became unrecognizable. You should try looking in the mirror and not knowing the reflection looking back at you. I long for the day I am able to look in the mirror and be OK with the person I see looking back.

Like all kids, when I was really young I used to think there was a monster in my closet and under my bed and you would come into my room and reassure me that there wasn't one by opening the closet and looking under the bed. Now that I am older you can't convince me of that anymore and it's not your job to. But since I found drugs I've come to the realization that there is a monster; but it's not in my closet or under the bed but inside of me, and that if I can't learn to ignore it, it will destroy me.

When I first started getting high it was pleasurable for a while; I had finally experienced nirvana, and then the euphoria wore off and I began to see the ugly side of my using and I experienced hell. I found the higher the drugs got me the lower they brought me. After a while I faced 2 choices, either I could suffer the pain of withdrawal or take more drugs. I did the withdrawal thing more times than you'll ever know and it's not pleasurable at all; in fact it's just the opposite. If you remember there were times where I said I couldn't go to school or work because I had the flu, but more times than not it was because I was going through withdrawal. I guess the best way to describe withdrawal is insuperable depression and acute anxiety — a drawn-out agony. Some of the times I choose [sic] withdrawal because I didn't want to use anymore, that I hated who I had become, but for the most part it was because I didn't have a choice in the matter...I had run out of drugs. You would think that after experiencing the emotional and physical pain of withdrawal that I would never let myself go through that again...right? See that's how you see it, but to me it just became a part of my using and a consequence I was willing to pay. You may call that insanity...I call that life.

I've been to enough meetings to know the readings by heart and one of the phrases that jumps out at me every time I hear it, is: "when we use drugs we are slowly committing suicide". I never thought of it that way but now I totally understand what it means...but still I use. I'm sure you remember the show Mash; it was pretty popular when you were growing up. The theme song is actually titled "suicide is painless" and in its context, I'm sure it's true. But the slow suicide of my using is not painless in the least; I feel the pain and can see the flame of my life getting fainter every time I use.

All those times you yelled at me for my using you gave me exactly what I needed to feed my addiction. You thought you were doing it out of love but you were actually justifying to me what my mind had convinced me I was a long time ago. I look at myself as a failure; as a complete waste of space. There is a line from a song called Southern Cross and this line defines my past and it goes: "I never failed to fail because it's the easiest thing to do." When you yell and scream you just confirm to me that I am a failure and after a while it becomes common place; not to mention expected. It is one thing if I think of myself as a loser or failure but to know that's how you see me as well makes it easier for my mind to convince me to use. My basic problem is that I flee from those who want me and I pursue my rejecters.

There are a few things you can do if you really want to help me. I know by telling you these things I'm actually cutting off my main money source...you. I will never stop using as long as you keep giving me money or supporting me. I can only stop using when I hit my bottom and only I can put down the shovel and quit digging.

When you bail me out, buy me a car, pay for my rent or give me money you aren't helping me at all; you are only handing me the shovel again and telling me to keep digging. You keep letting me come back home to live because you think you're helping me out but if your [sic] honest, you'll realize that you are doing it for purely selfish reasons. When you know I'm in the room next door you sleep better.

The last thing I'll confess to you is the real reason I steal from you. I steal from you because I'm counting on you not calling the cops on me. I count on you not wanting me to go to jail; to have a criminal record. I steal from you because you keep letting me move back home.

You make the mistake of thinking that recovery is simply a matter of not drinking or using drugs. And you consider a relapse a sign of complete failure and long periods of abstinence a complete success. But these perceptions are too simplistic. My life is anything but simple and I'm not just talking about my using drugs.

The way my mind works, nothing is as easy as just doing it because my mind tries to convince me not to do it. It doesn't matter how simple of a task it is…even unloading the dishwasher is a mind struggle for me. My mind also loves to make every little thing that goes wrong a major crisis.

Let me try to explain this in as simple terms as I possibly can. Let's say we both go outside in the morning and our cars don't start. You go in and call a mechanic and I go in and call suicide prevention. I'm what they call a W.C.S person; which stands for worst case scenario. They say a mind is a terrible thing to waste; well my mind is a terrible thing to listen to. Most people are about as happy as they make up their minds to be…mine won't let me be happy. My mind keeps reminding me that there is only 18 inches between a halo and a noose.

Relapse isn't a requirement but it does happen to quite a few addicts. The hard truth is that if there were 50 addicts in their 1st meeting together, more of us will be dead in 5 years then will have 5 years clean. The last time I relapsed it was because the bottom fell out faster than I could lower my standards. It's really difficult to solve a problem with the same mind that created it and God knows I've created a lot of problems for myself…and for you.

I hope someday you will realize that I am not a bad person trying to get good; I'm a sick person trying to get well. I suffer from the disease of addiction. If you believe this you won't be so critical of me. For a critic is just a person who goes onto the battlefield after the battle has been fought and shoots the survivors.

Believe me when I say this; I don't want to be an addict as much as you wish you weren't a parent of one.

I love you.

Sincerely,

Your loved one battling addiction (Author unknown)

Hope for the Broken Road

Part Three

Know There Is Hope

If not for my faith in Jesus Christ, I would forever be in a state of deep grief over how addiction has tried to destroy my family. As I dig my nails into Scripture, I am reminded of many truths. In the end, the evil of addiction does not win, Christ wins.

Amidst the intense sadness and chaos surrounding addiction there beams a ray of hope, a hope believing this is not all there is to this life. The Bible teaches us we will have many trials and tribulations in this life, and yet it tells us to be of good cheer, because Christ has overcome the world (John 16:33). Sometimes, addiction clouds the truth of God's Word and we begin to think God does not care or He is nowhere to be found. However, this is opposite of the Bible's teaching. God is there. He is with you. He has not abandoned you. He promises He will never leave you nor forsake you (Hebrews 13:5).

I have struggled just like you with my faith as I have watched my child self-destruct in addiction. I have cried out to God, asked Him to deliver her from herself, and begged Him not to let her die. Even though His Word promises grace, I have not always felt grace. I remember a time I was on the floor crying and praying. I had been reading 2 Corinthians 12:19. In this passage, God is speaking to the apostle Paul regarding an affliction Paul was experiencing. God told Paul, His (God's) grace was sufficient for Paul's affliction. As I read the passage and applied it to my life, God's grace did not feel sufficient for me in the brokenness I was experiencing regarding my adult child's addiction.

Through those many tears I learned a profound lesson: God's grace is not based on how I feel and His grace IS sufficient to carry me through this journey. Just as God's grace is sufficient for me, it is sufficient to see you through the grief of the broken road of your child's addiction. Even in the midst of the storm, there is hope.

Recently, I shared on my blog three things God has shown me through this ordeal. Here is an excerpt from my blog:

Grace- *God's word says His grace is sufficient, no matter what the outcome. I pray my child would know the depth of the love of God and turn to the One True God. But what if my child dies? "My grace is sufficient; my strength will be made perfect in your weakness." 2 Corinthians 12:9. I have had to learn even if my prayers are not answered the way I want, God is still good and His grace will see me through.*

Emotion- *God is not defined by an emotion. Whether you or I are anxious, sad, or depressed, God still reigns supreme. The story of the cross and redemption does not change because my emotions change. God is the same yesterday, today, and forever. He is immutable.*

Dependence- *God is dependable. No matter how much despair you or I feel, He can still be trusted. Why? Because His Word says He is good and trustworthy. God cannot go contrary to His Word. So if His word says he is good, then you and I have to take Him at His word. He will never leave us nor forsake us.*

As I am still walking the broken road of addiction with my child, sometimes my soul feels weary and tired. There are days I am overcome with helplessness and despair. During those times, I am reminded to keep my eyes gazed on Christ and to be continually before Him in prayer. I ask God to save my child from herself and to remove the veil over her heart so she can see Christ more clearly. I pray and meditate on Scripture, which has aided me in dealing with the difficulty of my child's addiction and the uncertainty surrounding her life. I have been strengthened and prodded to continue to persevere in the faith.

I encourage you to fight on your knees for your children. Put on the full armor of God, especially the sword of the Spirit which is the Word of God (Ephesians 6:10-17). Allow God to speak to your heart through His Word. Then, turn those passages into prayers. I have read and meditated on Ezekiel 37, the story of the dry bones. You can pray through the passage, *"God breathe life into my child; let her live again. Give her hope that she can live again through the power of God."*

I frequently use 2 Corinthians 3:12-15, asking God to remove the veil that covers the heart of my child, so she can see Christ clearly. As I pray Nehemiah 2, I ask God to rebuild the walls of my family that have been broken by addiction. There has been many a night I cried out Lamentations 2:19, pouring out my heart like water before God for my children.

No matter the outcome, no matter what happens, my heartfelt desire is for you to know God's grace is sufficient to see you through the brokenness. As Lamentations 3:22-24 states, we have a great promise of God's mercies being fresh and new every morning. Every. Single. Morning. My prayer for you, the parent of an addict just like me, is for the Lord to be your portion and your true hope would be found in the person of Jesus Christ. (Lamentations 3:24).

Epilogue

From the beginning of writing this book, my desire has been to help parents of addicts by sharing my own story of what I have learned on the broken road of addiction with my adult child. However, a vital link to the story is absent. There is so much more to write between these pages. I could not yet pen the words, because my heart is raw with unspeakable emotion and grief. This book chronicles my experience with my daughter, Lindsay, but I have also walked this road with my son, Gabriel. This book is dedicated to Gabriel, who was probably responsible for saving Lindsay's life, and yet just like Lindsay, Gabriel struggled with addiction.

Gabriel was not as fortunate as Lindsay. He overdosed with a combination of alcohol and heroin on April 8, 2013, and died four days later on April 12, 2013. This was truly one of the darkest days we have ever faced as a family. Our faith in God has been tested to its very depth.

We cannot walk along this broken road without asking what lies ahead for our loved ones and ourselves when our earthly bodies die. What about the resurrection? Is there truth in what the Bible teaches about the resurrection of Christ and the promise of a new life as seen in 1 Corinthians 15:12-20?

While having many questions about Gabriel's death, I turn to Scripture to find answers. What happens to believers who die? Paul, an apostle of Christ, answers this question in the Bible passage of 1 Thessalonians 4:13-18: God brings them back to life.

As I think about Gabriel, embedded forever in my mind is a

vision of him standing before his church proclaiming his belief in Christ, believing with his heart and confessing with his mouth his salvation in Jesus. I rejoice knowing God's Holy Spirit allowed Gabriel to believe and receive Christ (John 1:12). Gabriel received Christ and became a believer when he was fifteen years old.

I also rejoice because God made a way for Gabriel, through Christ, who became a sin offering, so in Him (Christ), Gabriel might become the righteousness of God. Christ exchanges his righteousness for our sin. Christ imputed His righteousness to my son. For this I am most thankful (2 Corinthians 5:21). And, I am eternally grateful because God sent His Son Jesus, so my son, Gabriel, could have life (John 3: 16). I know one day I will be with Gabriel in heaven when my time on this earth comes to an end.

I am learning many lessons on this trajectory about trust and hope in Christ. When my heart is ready and in God's timing, Gabriel's story will be shared with the lessons I have learned while on this journey with my family. We are learning to live without Gabriel's presence in this world. For now, we rest in the fact this world is not our true home and this is not where we belong.

I leave you with one last thought from Tim Keller, taken from his book *Walking With God Through Pain And Suffering* which has helped tremendously to soothe my grieving heart:

"But resurrection is not just consolation—it is restoration. We get it all back—the love, the loved ones, the goods, the beauties of this life—but in new, unimaginable degrees of glory and joy and strength" (59).

About the Author

Arlene lives in Louisville, Kentucky where she is Founder of *The Gabriel Project 930*, a drug addiction ministry reaching out to addicts, their families, and her community. She is a graduate of The Southern Baptist Theological Seminary in Louisville, Kentucky where she earned her Master of Divinity Degree in Christian Education with a concentration in Women's Leadership. Arlene served as the Women's Ministry Institute Consultant for Southern Seminary through the Women's Leadership Program from 2007-2011. During that time, Arlene's accomplishments include being a contributing author to two books: *The Hidden Person of the Heart: Discovering What God Says About and to Women Through the Scriptures* by Janet Wicker and *Women at Southern: A Walk Through Psalms* by Jaye Martin. She is married to Keith Rice, and has four grown children, Dana, Jacob, Gabriel, and Lindsay, and is Mimi to Joshua, Caleb, Emily, and Shaylynn.

You can learn more about Arlene and *The Gabriel Project 930* at http://gp930.com/.

Resources

BLOGS

Changing Lives Foundation
http://www.drug-addiction-help-now.org/

No Heroin in Heaven
http://noheroininheaven.com/

100 Pedals: Recovery for Parents Dealing with Addiction in Their Families
http://www.100pedals.com/

Parents Of An Addict
http://www.addictionjournal.org/pages/addiction-blogs

Parent Pathway
 http://parentpathway.com/

Sandy Swenson
http://www.sandyswenson.com/

Shatterproof
http://www.shatterproof.org/

BOOKS

Cataldi, Libby. 2010. *Stay Close: A Mother's Story of her Son's Addiction.* St. Martin's Griffin.

Conyers, Beverly. 2009. *An Addict in the Family: Stories of Loss, Hope, and Recovery*. Hazelden Publishing.

Herzenak, Joe. 2012 (Rev Upd edition). *Why Don't They Just Quit*. CreateSpace Independent Publishing Platform.

Keller, Timothy. 2013. *Walking with God through Pain and Suffering*. New York: Dutton Adult: Published by The Penguin Group.

Mansfield, Dennis, 2013. *Beautiful Nate; A Memoir of a Families Love, a Life Lost, and Heaven's Promises.* Howard Books.

Rice, Arlene. 2014. *Parent of an Adult Addict: Hope for the Broken Road*. CreateSpace Independent Publishing Platform.

Speakman, Michael. 2014. *The Four Seasons of Recovery: For Parents of Alcoholics and Addicts*. Phoenix: Rite of Passage Press.

Swenson, Sandy. 2014 (Release Date September 9). *The Joey Song: A Mother's Story of her Son's Addiction*. Central Recovery Press.

Wandzilak, Kristina. 2006. *The Lost Years: Surviving a Mother and Daughter's Worst Nightmare*. Jeffers Press.

Welch, Edward T. 2001. *Addictions: A Banquet in the Grave: Finding Hope in the Power of the Gospel*. Phillipsburg: P&R Publishing.

LEGISLATION, INTERVENTION LAWS, & RESEARCH

Casey's Law (Kentucky & Ohio)
http://caseyslaw.org/KY_Files/About.htm

Jennifer Act (Indiana & Florida)
 http://thejenniferact.com/

McLellan, A. Thomas: CEO & Co- Founder, Treatment Research Institute
 http://www.tresearch.org/index.php/our-people/executive-team/

Network for Public Health Law: (Good Samaritan & Naloxone Laws by State)
https://www.networkforphl.org/_asset/qz5pvn/network-naloxone.pdf

People Advocating Recovery (PAR)
http://www.peopleadvocatingrecovery.org/

People Advocating Recovery Northern Kentucky (PAR NKY)
http://drugfreenky.org/people-advocating-for-recovery/

Treatment Research Institute
http://www.tresearch.org/

PARENT COACHES

Herzenak, Joe (provides telephone sessions): Changing Lives Foundation.
http://www.drug-addiction-help-now.org/about-changing-lives-foundation/about-changing-lives-foundation-and-joe-judy-herzanek

Light House Network (Ongoing coaching for parents of addicts, phone help available)
http://lighthousenetwork.org/

Speakman, Michael, L.I.S.A.C., Speakman Coaching and Consulting (Provides telephone sessions as well as free monthly telephone parent group sessions)
mikespeakman.com/

FACEBOOK SUPPORT

Addiction Journal
https://www.facebook.com/AddictionJournal

Celebrate Recovery®
https://www.facebook.com/celebraterecovery

Heroin Doesn't Care
https://www.facebook.com/heroindoesntcare

No Longer Bound
https://www.facebook.com/nolongerbound

Operation 6:12
https://www.facebook.com/Operation612

PAR NKY (People Advocating Recovery Northern Kentucky)
https://www.facebook.com/nkpar

Teen Challenge
https://www.facebook.com/pages/Teen-Challenge/112909512056974

The Addicts Mom
https://www.facebook.com/addictsmom

The Addicts Mom: KY State Chapter
https://www.facebook.com/groups/TamKentuckyChapter/

SUPPORT GROUPS

Al-Anon®
http://al-anon.alateen.org/home

Celebrate Recovery®
http://www.celebraterecovery.com/

Families Anonymous® (Group Meetings by State)
http://www.familiesanonymous.org/image/data/WSOF-07%20US-Mtg-Dir%202014-01B.pdf

Grief Share Support Groups (groups can be found in many cities)
http://www.griefshare.org/

Nar-anon®
http://www.nar-anon.org/naranon/About_Nar-Anon

Parents of Addicted Loved Ones (PAL Groups)
http://palgroup.squarespace.com/

The Addicts Mom
http://addictsmom.com/

TREATMENT LOCATORS AND HELP

Affordable Care Act (If your adult child needs insurance):
http://www.healthcaremarketplace.com/'?on=enr&gclid=CMeXrPyE
1/8CFQg0aQodGQoAlg

American Heart Association (Learn CPR)
http://www.heart.org/HEARTORG/CPRAndECC/CPR_UCM_0011
18_SubHomePage.jsp

American Red Cross (Learn CPR)
http://www.redcross.org/lp/cpr-aed-firstaid

Belle Grove Springs (Residential treatment for men, Kentucky)
http://www.bellegrovesprings.com/

Free Rehab Centers
http://www.freerehabcenters.org/

Help Guide: What to Look for When Choosing a Drug Treatment Program
http://www.helpguide.org/mental/choosing_drug_rehab_treatment.ht
m

Intervention America: National Resource on Recovery (Locator for treatment help)
http://soberliving.interventionamerica.org/

Isaiah's House (Men & Women detox & residential treatment, Kentucky. Only facility in nation using NET for detox)
http://isaiah-house.org/

Jefferson Alcohol and Drug Addiction Center (JADAC, Low Cost Medical Detox 24 hour hotline)
http://www.sevencounties.org/poc/view_doc.php?type=doc&id=24361

Karen's Place (Residential women, VOUCHERS AVAILABLE, Louisa, KY)
http://www.karensplace.com/

Naloxone (FAQ)
http://www.stopoverdose.org/faq.htm

National Institute on Drug Abuse: (NIDA)
http://www.drugabuse.gov/

No Longer Bound (Men Faith Based, Cumming, Ga.)
http://nolongerbound.com/

Operation 6: 12 (FREE, Men Faith Based Ohio)
https://www.facebook.com/Operation612

Opioid Overdose Prevention and Education
http://www.stopoverdose.org/index.htm

Recovery Connection Help
http://www.recoveryconnection.org/

Second Chances Outreach Center (Men's residential, faith based, Kentucky)
http://2ndchanceoutreach.com/

Sober-Solutions: 1-888-762-3730 (Will provide free phone help sessions)
http://www.sober-solutions.com/recovery-counselor/

Substance Abuse and Mental Health Administration (SAMHA): 1-800-662-HELP (4357)
http://findtreatment.samhsa.gov/TreatmentLocator/faces/quickSearch.jspx

Teen Challenge (Men and Women Faith Based, Inpatient)
http://teenchallengeusa.com/

Transitions, Inc. (Men and Women, Northern KY)
http://www.transitionsky.org/our-services

The Healing Place (FREE: Men and Women Non- Medical Detox and Inpatient, Louisville, Ky)
http://www.thehealingplace.org/

The Partnership® at DrugFree.Org
http://www.drugfree.org/

VIDEOS

Cataldi, Libby: Stay Close
https://www.youtube.com/watch?v=u2O7fCRRx0I

Herzenak, Joe: Why Don't They Just Quit
https://www.whydonttheyjustquit.com/index.php?route=product/product&path=61&product_id=54

Keller, Timothy: Walking with God through Pain and Suffering
http://timothykeller.com/books/walking_with_god_through_pain_and_suffering/

NBC: Why Rehab Doesn't Work (Parts 1-4 with Treatment Research Institute Co-Founder A. Thomas McLellan, PhD)

Video 1
http://www.nbcnews.com/video/nbcnews.com/54858657#54858657

Video 2
http://www.nbcnews.com/video/nbcnews.com/54858658#54858658

Video 3
http://www.nbcnews.com/video/nbcnews.com/54858659#54858659

Video 4
http://www.nbcnews.com/watch/nbcnews-com/why-rehab-doesnt-work-part-4-215533123538

Speakman, Michael: How to Help an Addicted Loved One
http://vimeo.com/40164529

The Anonymous People
http://vimeo.com/ondemand/theanonymouspeople/87754462?gclid=CNfai-q49L0CFc9AMgodYDQA3g

Wandzilak, Kristina (Full Circle Interventionist, On Drug Addiction and Rehabilitation)
http://fullcircleintervention.com/post/video-kristina-wandzilak-on-drug-addiction-and-rehabilitation.php

41695738R00050

Made in the USA
Lexington, KY
22 May 2015